SMALL GROUP
ToolBox

BUILDING CHARACTER
THROUGH TESTING TIMES

Ron Kallmier

CONTENTS

PREFACE

In this series of four studies we will be considering the nature of trials, temptations and troubles that invade our lives as followers of Jesus Christ and how they can be used by God to achieve a very positive result. We can recognise that some of the trials and troubles we face are our own fault but many come unexpected and unwelcome into our everyday lives. Temptations are certainly trials but the difference is that temptations pull us towards sinful behaviour. The power of temptations is that they are very attractive to us. Temptations may range from simply unwise enticements, such as eating too much cake, or they may draw us into immoral, unethical, illegal or ungodly behaviour. Trials and troubles are things we would rather avoid. How we manage each of these three – trials, troubles and temptations – will determine whether we grow in character or become trapped in unhealthy thoughts, emotions and behaviour.

Over recent months I have been drawn to consider more closely the three temptations of Jesus as recorded in the Gospels of Matthew and Luke. I was trying to understand more deeply what Jesus experienced and how He was able to remain true to His heavenly Father through them all. In the process other scriptures came to mind and added to my understanding. It became so much clearer to me – He really does understand our trials and temptations. He really did everything possible to identify with us. Because of His understanding of our humanity He truly does forgive us completely and welcome us warmly both into His family and into His friendship. He is not surprised or dismayed at our failures because He has provided a way out of every failure through His death and resurrection. He views our trials and temptations as opportunities for us to achieve growth and greatness in His kingdom.

In these reflections on the earthly life of Jesus I recalled the prophetic words of Isaiah found in chapter 53 of his book. Isaiah accurately portrays the life of the coming Messiah. It was not to be one of royalty and pageantry but rather of trials and immense suffering.

And so it was. When we sketch a timeline of the earthly life of our Lord Jesus Christ, what do we find? He was born into the humblest circumstance of His day. His life was immediately in jeopardy as King Herod tried to snuff Him out in His early months. To escape the death threats He and His family became refugees in Egypt. On His return to Israel, He lived in the reviled region of Galilee. From the beginning of His public ministry He was ridiculed and opposed by those who despised His power and feared His message. For three years He suffered all manner of temptations in addition to the stress of His public ministry. Eventually, after enduring these three years of personal trials that we cannot even imagine, He was falsely accused and crucified as a common criminal by the religious bigots of His day. At His lowest point He was deserted by His disciples. He suffered the full spectrum of the agony of a mock trial and was crucified. He endured unimaginable physical and spiritual torment as the brutality of His unjust treatment was compounded by the sin of the ages that He took on Himself.

Isaiah put it so well when he prophesied some 700 years previously: 'He was ... a man of sorrows, acquainted with bitterest grief' (Isaiah 53:3). Yet He was never defeated and He never surrendered in those trials. Without wavering Jesus did what His heavenly Father desired and as planned He rose triumphantly from the tomb.

In hindsight we know that the agonies He experienced had a profound purpose. In the middle of His suffering He looked ahead to the joy that was coming. Hebrews 12:1–3 summarises this so well. While considering these verses I asked myself: Can I look beyond my current trials and believe that there can be a positive and highly desirable outcome for me? Can you?

Compared to the trial and crucifixion, we may think that the testing in the wilderness may have been easier for Jesus. Of course, it was not. He struggled with a pull of options that offered Him a less painful way ahead. It was an attractive alternative to submission to the divine plan that would bring us back into relationship with His Father. As we shall consider more fully later, He was tested (or tempted) in the same areas that each of us are tempted. The difference is that He did not falter. He did not fail. Not once.

At the heart of this study book is an invitation to explore this unique experience of testing in the wilderness. It is my prayer that by grappling with the trials of Jesus, we can discover something that will help us in our own journey through our own unique trials and temptations. Together in your groups you may discover better ways of coming through trials victoriously and growing as a person.

Ron Kallmier, 2014

SUGGESTIONS FOR USING THIS STUDY GUIDE

SUGGESTION FOR SMALL GROUP LEADERS

- As far possible keep discussions practically orientated, including the Bible study section each week.

- Many of the suggestions for individuals and groups are quite meaty and you may find that you only cover one of these in a group session. That is OK.

- Encourage the group members to do some preparation for the following week. Their best preparation may be as simple as thinking over how they respond to the questions or issues featured in each study.

- Group members will be very different in the terms of trials and temptations that each one of them faces. Exploring the mystery of the wilderness temptations of Jesus will potentially raise many questions about their own life experiences.

- The group times will be the most effective if there is integrity and honesty in the discussion. Some groups trust each other enough to explore real, deeper issues of personal temptation or their reactions to personal struggles that some are experiencing. It is the leader who will set the best example and be the best encourager of openness within the group.

- There are four parts to each of the studies in this book. The first is the Preview, which briefly introduces the set topic. Next is Personal Exploration, guiding personal study and reflection. Third, Studying Together provides questions and suggestions for study of the Bible passages within a small group context. Finally, Applying the Scriptures offers some thought-provoking questions about practical issues involved in building character today.

- Of course, you are free to use the suggestions in any way that fits your own group best. While the book is designed for four small group sessions, you may find it best to use some of the suggestions, discard others and add your own also. Allocate as many group sessions as you believe are necessary to cover this important topic.

- It is recommended that you address real questions and real issues from within the group whenever this is appropriate. Sessions are not intended to be simply a theoretical discussion, but very practical.

- In a healthy group environment, positive experiences, and any uncertainties or concerns of group members will surface. This openness will stimulate frank and open exploration of the issues raised.

- Ideally, group members should complete the series with greater confidence in God's presence with them and encouragement that even in the darkest of our experiences God can produce good for us and in us.

- By the way, we suggest you don't pressure anyone to be involved in the discussion if they appear unwilling. Make space for individuals to process their own thoughts and to consider what others are saying.

SUGGESTIONS FOR YOUR PERSONAL USE

- The study series aims to apply biblical experiences and teaching to the everyday life experiences of individual Christians.

- In addition to the spaces provided in this study book, you may find it useful to get hold of a small journal or notebook to use during the period of time that you are focusing on this topic. Here are some things you may like to jot down and question as you look at this topic:

  –Why was the period of wilderness temptation necessary?
  –What did it achieve?
  –What can we learn from it today?
  –If God is a God of love, why does He allow us to go through the suffering that so many of us experience?
  –Why do some people seem to have it easier than I do?
  –Does God have favourites?
  –How can I learn to look beyond my present difficulties and search for the positive outcome that God has in mind?

  We will return to some of these questions later.

PRACTICAL SUGGESTIONS FOR SMALL GROUPS

- If you plan to use the book in a small group, it is recommended that group members read the Preview, and spend some time in personal preparation for the next group meeting. With our busy lives, this will be quite a challenge for some or possibly the entire group, but the preparation will help to give maximum benefit to the group members.

- This series provides a great opportunity to hear the life stories of each person in the group. Some may express their emotional pain of deep loss at points during their lives. Others will show their confusion about the meaning of the trials they are facing. Some others may doubt that God really loves them and they may be trying to keep a safe distance from Him. The experiences or reactions of each individual should be valued and accepted. Sensitive listening by all group members will encourage honest sharing.

I pray that you will be blessed in your journey together as group.

INTRODUCTION

Have you ever wondered why the Holy Spirit led Jesus into the wilderness to be tested immediately after His baptism? He went from the profoundly affirming experience of water baptism and Spirit empowerment, accompanied by the thundering voice of His heavenly Father, to the inhospitable environment of the wilderness. Was this necessary? What was the purpose of this solitude and struggle?

At the heart of the three temptations of Jesus recorded in the Gospels is a diabolical strategy that aimed to promote self-dependence rather than God-dependence; self-focus rather than other-focus. The fate of all humankind depended on how Jesus, who was God in the flesh, addressed these very real challenges.

When we look more closely at the wilderness temptations we realise that they were a strategic attempt to undermine both the identity and destiny of the Son of God. This same approach had worked previously with the human race (Gen. 3) and it remains so effective today. The plan did not succeed with Jesus Christ. It would be wrong to believe that these were the only temptations that Jesus faced. The enemy's assault on Him was relentless and yet Jesus never wavered. He always put His heavenly Father's will first. He knew what the outcome of His voluntary submission to suffering and death would be.

But why was it necessary for Jesus to be tempted? In fact, why was it necessary for Him to come to earth as a human being in the first place? The Son of God's mission on earth was to open the way for fallen human beings to be restored into intimate relationship with His Father. This was the most astounding outcome for people like you and me.

In Jesus Christ there was once more a human being on planet Earth who would demonstrate how to overcome the strategies of the evil one. Of course, Jesus is the Son of God and He did not need any refining or purifying for Himself, but as the writer to the Hebrews says, He is 'the author and perfecter of our faith' (Heb. 12:2, NIV).

It is worth noting that the very first sin was committed because the first humans believed the lies and followed the path away from God and from His best plans for their lives (Gen. 3). Jesus, the last Adam, through His sweat, blood and pain, rejected the lies and deceit, taking back everything that the enemy had stolen through the original strategy of deception and lies that had subtly but radically infiltrated the first humans.

Yes, Adam's one sin brought condemnation upon everyone, but Christ's one act of righteousness makes all people right in God's sight and gives them life. Because one person disobeyed God, many people became sinners. But because one other person obeyed God, many people will be made right in God's sight.
(Rom. 5:18–19)

So it is written: 'The first man Adam became a living being'; the last Adam, a life-giving spirit.
(1 Cor. 15:45, NIV)

Our human identity and destiny was stolen but it has now been restored through the cross and resurrection. Through His self-sacrifice we have been able to escape our guilt and find forgiveness and freedom. We have regained our identity as God's masterpiece and once again we are empowered by the Holy Spirit to achieve all that God had prepared in advance for each of us to do. How amazing!

*And so God can always point to us as examples of the incredible wealth of his favor and kindness toward us, as shown in all he has done for us through Christ Jesus. God saved you by his special favor when you believed. And you can't take credit for this; it is a gift from God. Salvation is not a reward for the good things we have done, so none of us can boast about it. For we are God's masterpiece. **He has created us anew in Christ Jesus, so that we can do the good things he planned for us long ago**.*
(Eph. 2:7–10, emphasis mine)

Now let's be honest. Even as Christians we have to admit that in the past God's ways have not always held the central place in our lives. Trials and temptations often make this problem come into clearer focus because in these difficult times we find that our resources and our wisdom are insufficient. One reason God allows us to go through testing times is to draw us back into His grace and mercy; to lead our lives back onto His path.

How this works to our benefit is beautifully illustrated in Malachi 3:1–4, a passage that describes the messenger of the new covenant. Malachi paints a prophetic picture of the ancient way of refining silver. His focus is on the refiner and his task. The refiner's primary function was to oversee the level of heat that was applied to the melting silver. The perfect temperature allowed the dross (the rubbish) to rise to the surface and be skimmed off by the refiner, without overheating the silver in the process. Just enough heat but not too much so that the silver would become as pure as possible. Trials can have the same outcome if we allow them to do so.

Let's be clear. God does not tempt anyone, as the letter of James points out:

> *When tempted, no one should say, 'God is tempting me.' For God cannot be tempted by evil, nor does he tempt anyone.*
> (James 1:13, NIV)

Nevertheless God can use the enemy's worst attacks to refine our character and produce good in us and through us if our hearts are sensitive to the presence of the Holy Spirit, purifying, guiding, strengthening, and encouraging us. If we do this we receive God's blessings and gain His 'well done!'. Our Christian character grows and God receives the glory. Jesus said:

> *Here on earth you will have many trials and sorrows. But take heart, because I have overcome the world.*
> (John 16:33)

PART ONE

MAKE THESE STONES INTO BREAD

FOCUS PASSAGES:

MATTHEW 4:1–4; LUKE 4:1–4

PREVIEW

It is interesting that this temptation – the first recorded in both Matthew and Luke – relates to food. So did the first temptation recorded in Genesis 3. I guess the stones did not look as appetising as the fruit in the Garden of Eden but that was not the point. The central issue in both temptations was how they responded to what God said. Food is important but attending to what God says is far more important. Obedience has always been central to a close relationship with Him.

So what was this temptation designed to do? In part, at least, it was designed to pressure Jesus into ignoring His humanity and to operate out of His divinity. If the tactic had been successful it would have undermined the strategic divine plan described by the apostle Paul:

> *Though he [Jesus] was God, he did not demand and cling to his rights as God. He made himself nothing; he took the humble position of a slave and appeared in human form. And in human form he obediently humbled himself even further by dying a criminal's death on a cross.*
> (Phil. 2:6-8)

Scriptural passages such as this one reveal that the divine plan was to retrace the fallen steps of humanity and to redeem (buy back) the

human race from slavery to sin. Jesus, God's Son, did this by willingly taking human form on earth. There was now a Man on earth who lived perfectly in the way that God planned. Not only did Jesus live His life as God intended, but through His death and resurrection He shattered the chains forged by human sin and declared us 'not guilty' before His heavenly Father. In the process, Jesus opened the way for us to be restored into right relationship with God. What an amazing outcome!

However there is another strategy behind this first test. It is found in the opening word, 'if': 'If you are the Son of God' (Luke 4:3). With Jesus at the point of physical exhaustion, His body spent and aching for food, the enemy attempted to plant seeds of doubt about who He was – His identity as God's Son. Just as he did in the very first temptation in Eden, the enemy came with doubt, deception and distortion. He has used these devices from the beginning of human history and he still uses the same tactics with us today. Notice that the first seed of doubt he planted in Genesis 3 was in the form of the proposition that God was not good. He argued that God was holding back something desirable when He prohibited Adam and Eve from eating the fruit from just one tree (Gen. 3:1–5).

Perhaps you too have asked the questions: Am I really God's child? Has He really accepted and forgiven me? What if God has decided not to care for me?

Do you see the similarities here? Seeds of doubt may produce ungodly fruit. When we doubt the goodness of God and our status as His children we are inevitably thrown back onto our own resources.

Jesus may have been spent physically but His sense of identity was never shaken. He knew He was God's Son – no ifs and no buts. For us too, when we are physically and emotionally spent and we are battered and beaten by life's tough experiences, it is essential that we hold on to our understanding that we are definitely and unchangeably God's children.

Another critical issue surfaces in this first temptation of Jesus. It brings our essential life needs under the microscope. Let's be honest: each of us, at some level, desires basic things out of life. We have a deep desire for *security*. Security includes feeling safe from danger, having somewhere to live, having sufficient income to provide food and drink, clothing to wear, and so on. Many believers around the world live without security in any of these areas. Perhaps you are struggling with some of these needs right now. We also long for *significance*. We want our life to have purpose and meaning. We crave self-worth. Deep down we don't want to be nobodies who simply pass through life unnoticed and unvalued. *Hope* is also important. Hope keeps us going forward when things in the present are particularly tough. Hebrews 11 contains accounts of many people who, even though in dire circumstances, were sustained and motivated by their faith and hope.

> *By faith these people overthrew kingdoms, ruled with justice, and received what God had promised them. They shut the mouths of lions, quenched the flames of fire, and escaped death by the edge of the sword. Their weakness was turned to strength. They became strong in battle and put whole armies to flight. Women received their loved ones back again from death. But others trusted God and were tortured, preferring to die rather than turn from God and be free. They placed their hope in the resurrection to a better life.*
> (Heb. 11:33–35)

There is nothing at all wrong with pursuing any of these basic needs. A problem does arise however when they separate us from our faithful walk with God. Then we have some tough choices to make. For each one of us there will be situations when we must choose to walk God's way or the world's way. The choice that Jesus made is clear. What about our choices?

PERSONAL EXPLORATION

1. Spend time meditating on the words of Jesus: 'Man does not live on bread alone, but on every word that comes from the mouth of God' (Matt. 4:4, NIV). What would be the personal challenge or pressure that you would put in the place of the word 'bread'? If you are willing, begin with your name and reshape this sentence so that it is a strong personal statement of faith in and commitment to God.

(Your name) _____ does not live by _____ alone but by _____

2. Notice that Jesus did not ignore His physical needs in His response to this temptation. He recognised the importance of the necessities of life, but He also understood His correct priorities. Take a few minutes to consider the matters that have priority in your own life currently. Do you see any need to rearrange these priorities? If so, what would the changes look like?

3. Have you been challenged about your trust in God from the Scriptures recently? How have you responded? (See Matt. 6:25–34.)

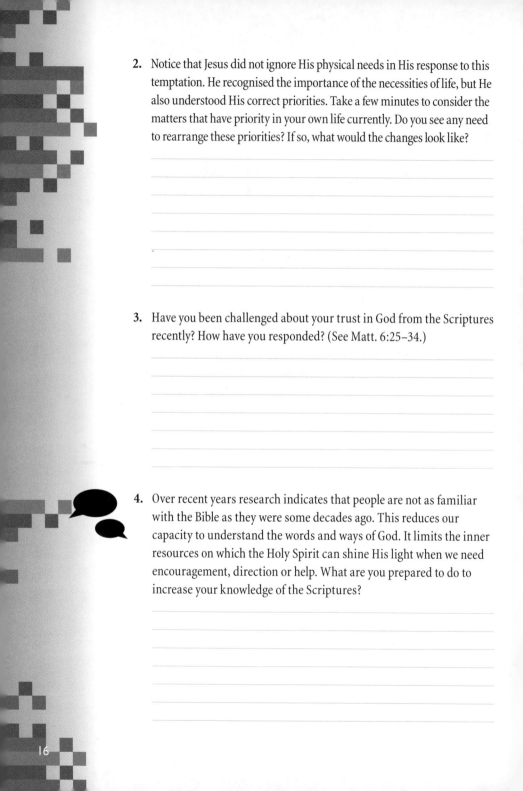

4. Over recent years research indicates that people are not as familiar with the Bible as they were some decades ago. This reduces our capacity to understand the words and ways of God. It limits the inner resources on which the Holy Spirit can shine His light when we need encouragement, direction or help. What are you prepared to do to increase your knowledge of the Scriptures?

STUDYING TOGETHER

The book of Hebrews gives us many insights into God's plan to redeem people. What do you discover in the passages below about the meaning of Jesus Christ's redeeming ministry on earth?

1. Hebrews 2:14–18

2. Hebrews 4:14–16

What occurs when people put their own ideas and plans above the specific commands of God? Here are some historical examples for the group to explore. What is the most significant warning or encouragement in each passage for you?

3. 1 Samuel 15:12–23

4. John 13:34–35

_____

_____

_____

_____

_____

_____

5. Revelation 2:1–7

_____

_____

_____

_____

_____

APPLYING THE SCRIPTURES

1. Throughout the world today there are people who face a stark choice
when it comes to keeping God central in their lives. Many face the
loss of essential things such as their work, their homes, or the safety
of their family. For some, their faith even costs them their lives. We
may be safe from this kind of persecution, but what can we learn from
their courageous example?

_____

_____

_____

_____

_____

_____

2. How can we continue to make wise life decisions when God appears to be distant? What have people in the group discovered about this? What part does your knowledge of the Scriptures play in those times when God's direction is unclear?

3. The physical hunger Jesus experienced was very powerful and urgent; however, He was able to keep His priorities right. Are there any of our own powerful and urgent needs or desires that may tempt us to ignore God's rightful priority in our lives?

4. Has someone you have known in the past taken dodgy shortcuts in order to meet personal desires or goals, doing things that were uncaring, unethical or illegal. What were the consequences? What did you learn from their experience? (Remember to protect confidentiality if the information you share is not common knowledge.)

PART TWO:

DON'T TEST THE LORD YOUR GOD

FOCUS PASSAGES:

MATTHEW 4:5–7; LUKE 4:9–12

PREVIEW

This is one test that I personally would find it easy to resist. Balancing on the edge of a steep drop over the side of the temple is not my idea of excitement. I can muster up some vertigo if I think about it long enough. To jump off in the belief that God would send angels to catch me before I thumped on the ground below … I don't think so!

But this is not about you or me. This was a very real temptation for the Son of God. He had angels who certainly would have responded if He had jumped. Unlike anyone else, however, Jesus understood His earthly destiny. He knew the cost and the pain involved in doing things His Father's way. He was also supremely confident in the unlimited resources of heaven that were available to Him at any time. Despite this, He remained focused on what His death and resurrection would accomplish. Remember how He agonised in the garden, asking the Father to take away the cross if there was any other way to achieve the divine plan. Through the deceitfulness of the evil one, another way was being offered here. It went like this: 'You claim that you are the Son of God. Prove it to yourself and prove it to the nation of Israel. Jump! You know what the Scriptures say. You are protected. Nothing can happen to you. Angels will make sure of that.'

To add weight to the deception, the devil added a passage of Scripture (Psa. 91:11–12).

Two obvious problems stand out in this temptation. First, this was not in God's plan and Jesus had committed Himself to do only what the Father said. The second problem was that it would be putting God to the test – something we have been commanded not to do (see for example Heb. 3:7–11). The word translated 'testing' carries the idea of testing God's patience beyond the limits. Jesus easily discerned that what was being asked of Him by Satan would dishonour God and simply draw attention to Himself in a way that He totally rejected.

Let's think for a while about the difference between testing God and proving that God is faithful by trusting Him. A great example of both is found in Malachi 3. By the prophetic voice of Malachi (vv6–9), God confronts the rebellion of the people who returned to Israel after the captivity in Babylon had ended (mid fifth century BC). Their actions were testing God. The particular sin that God focuses on among many others is their failure to give their tithes and offerings. This brought the whole nation under a curse. God's patience was almost at an end but He gave them one more opportunity to prove His faithfulness (vv10–12). Proving God's faithfulness is on God's terms and under God's instructions. That's the way it still works today. It is not wrong to prove God's faithfulness and love for us by acts of trusting Him, but we do this in ways that He has approved of in the Bible.

OUR TEMPTATIONS

Notice that the words, 'If you are the Son of God' are repeated in this temptation. As if Jesus could doubt who He was. But what about us: have we ever had doubts about God's existence or perhaps about our relationship with Him? These doubts can become toxic. They lead some people to come up with some crazy ideas, trying to prove that God is real, or that His love for them is genuine. I have known some Christians who have come up with some uninspired ways of finding God's will. Sadly, some of these experiments had very unhappy consequences. One of the reasons is that individuals have seized control of their lives and not relied upon what God has promised through His Word.

Probably you and I have never been tempted to jump over a cliff to prove that God is there and that He loves us. But if we are deeply honest with ourselves, do we allow our doubts to dominate our faith or to keep us living 'safely'? Do we try to keep our lives safe and predictable at all times, always within our control, avoiding risky steps of faith in God? Our drive

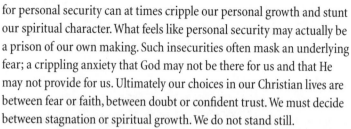

for personal security can at times cripple our personal growth and stunt our spiritual character. What feels like personal security may actually be a prison of our own making. Such insecurities often mask an underlying fear; a crippling anxiety that God may not be there for us and that He may not provide for us. Ultimately our choices in our Christian lives are between fear or faith, between doubt or confident trust. We must decide between stagnation or spiritual growth. We do not stand still.

The disciple Thomas was very much a 'seeing is believing' type of person. His feeling was that 'unless I see I won't believe that Jesus has risen from the dead'. How stunned Thomas was when Jesus appeared to him in the upper room and invited him to prove to himself that Jesus was alive. What Jesus said next is particularly relevant for us:

> *Then he said to Thomas, 'Put your finger here and see my hands. Put your hand into the wound in my side. Don't be faithless any longer. Believe!' 'My Lord and my God!' Thomas exclaimed. Then Jesus told him, 'You believe because you have seen me. **Blessed are those who haven't seen me and believe anyway.'***
> (John 20:27–29, emphasis mine)

May God grant us every day the kind of belief of that trusts His presence with us and His goodness towards us.

 ## PERSONAL EXPLORATION

1. Would you describe yourself as a 'seeing is believing' Christian? Consider how this influences your daily life.

2. Can you recall any times when God provided your needs when you were under considerable pressure? How did this influence your faith?

3. Take some time to consider Psalm 34. This psalm was forged in the fires of some very tough life experiences. What encouragement do you find here? Why not jot down your discoveries and use them as a basis for prayer.

STUDYING TOGETHER

Hebrews 3:7–19 (focus passage); Exodus 17:1–7; Numbers 16 (background reading).

1. In what ways did the Israelites test God?

2. Based on Hebrews 3:7–19, how could we recognise if a person has developed a hard heart towards God? What would be the symptoms? What could you do to help them if the opportunity arises?

3. Are you aware of any times when God has given you guidance but you have failed to follow through because of fear, uncertainty or a sense of inadequacy? What is your response now?

4. On occasions our anxieties and doubts tend to overwhelm us. Discuss the relevance of Psalm 139:23–24 with group members. Why not close with prayer for one another.

APPLYING THE SCRIPTURES

1. We notice in the temptation accounts that Jesus used Scripture to stand against the enemy. But we also observe that our enemy attacked with Scripture. How can we decide whether a particular passage of Scripture is relevant in our own lives at a particular time?

2. How can we help each other to make wise use of the Bible and avoid using passages of Scripture out of context?

3. Invite group members to share what it was that convinced them to believe in and follow Jesus Christ.

4. Many Christians go through seasons of doubt. Perhaps some individuals in your group have been there or are in one of those seasons right now. Take time to listen to each other's stories and then to encourage and pray for one another.

PART THREE

WORSHIP THE LORD YOUR GOD AND SERVE HIM ONLY

FOCUS PASSAGES

MATTHEW 4:8–11; LUKE 4:5–8

PREVIEW
The temptations Jesus faced

The heavenly agreement that Christ would come to redeem and rescue humanity was at stake here. It was a test of obedience, of commitment to follow the path of His earthly destiny. Of course the devil would not have understood the divine plan because he is not all-knowing, but he did realise that something was coming and he did everything he could to derail it. The challenge to kneel down and worship the devil was another devious trick that offered Jesus a short-cut to reclaiming His rightful place as ruler among the world's peoples and empires. But how great was the price and how evil the consequences would have been. Each of us would have remained eternally lost if Jesus had weakened at this point. In a sense the outcome was never in doubt. Jesus was totally committed to the Father's will. I really like the way He takes control and, in modern speech, He tells the devil to get lost. He affirms that God alone is to be worshipped and that is where His commitment will remain – a rock solid commitment.

Implications for us

When we limit worship to what we do in a congregation on Sundays we miss the whole idea that the Scripture implies. Worship is a whole-of-life orientation. Worship flows out of the way we set our hearts, our will and our actions.

The crucial test is always to do with who or what we worship. If we are God's children there is only room for Him in the centre of our hearts, though this does not exclude love for family, friends and others we meet. We can discover the centre of our worship by recognising the person(s) or thing(s) that occupy the core of our being (our hearts). It's what drives us and what dominates us. When everything else is stripped away, what gives our life its ultimate meaning and purpose? Essentially we *are* worshipping beings and what we worship we serve – with time, money, energy and passion, as we shall see later.

Some people live with an aching emptiness deep within. Their need for worship is suppressed by all the troubles and pain of their lives. They do the best they can to block out this pain. Deep down they find life to be meaningless. How tragic. Others have clearly chosen to worship something or someone other than God.

Why is what we worship so important, so crucial? It is because we are designed by God to be *imaging* creatures (Gen. 1:26–27). That is, we were created to both *reflect* and absorb the qualities of what we worship – God Himself. God has designed us to be transformed more and more into His image as we spend time with Him (1 John 3:1–3; 2 Cor. 3:16–18). What an amazing thought! Moses experienced something of this during his unique time with God on the mountain in Sinai. The result of his lengthy encounter with the Almighty was that his face shone with the reflected glory of God (Exod. 34:29–35).

We also *absorb* from the world we live in. The most obvious example is the food we eat. A healthy diet makes us strong while a poor diet weakens us physically and intellectually. We are also influenced by the environment in which we live and those people with whom we interact, for better or for worse. I remember an old story about a woman who went to tour a coal mine in a white dress. She asked the tour guide if she could wear her white dress down the coal mine. He replied that she certainly could but that it would not be white when she came out. Our environment does impact us. If we have endured a painful or deprived early life the effects on us may continue for many years, perhaps throughout our lives. As adults, what we allow into our minds and spirits also influences the strength of our character and our spiritual wellbeing.

We take on board (absorb) these experiences and the consequences of our choices so that they become part of who we are. The good news is that we can change. We can also choose to avoid many harmful elements in our personal worlds and to react in a godly way to those experiences and people that are potentially damaging to us.

So here is the critical issue: if we turn away from worshipping God we will desire to worship something else or someone else. The Bible condemns this as idolatry. The Old Testament is full of warnings against the many consequences of idolatry. Psalm 115:1–8 is very clear on this. Look particularly at the following verses, describing idols that the people had made:

> *They have mouths, but cannot speak, eyes, but they cannot see; they have ears, but cannot hear, noses, but they cannot smell; they have hands, but cannot feel, feet, but they cannot walk; nor can they utter a sound with their throats.* **Those who make them will be like them, and so will all who trust in them.**
>
> (Psa. 115:5–8, NIV, emphasis mine)

Psalm 135:15–18 echoes the same thoughts. We are transformed by what we worship. G.K. Beale repeatedly emphasises, 'We resemble what we revere, either for ruin or restoration.'[1]

Israel and Judah turned away so easily from the worship of God to the idols of the surrounding nations. They took on characteristics of the idols they served; namely, blindness and deafness and hardness of heart (Isa. 6). In the physical realm we understand the severe problems that blindness, deafness and hardening of the arteries causes people. The problems become even more acute in our spiritual natures because idolatry cuts people off from the very source of their spiritual lives. The difference between the physical and the spiritual conditions is that the spiritual condition is a result of personal choice – a very dangerous choice indeed. This spiritual condition is not easily recognised. The consequences of turning away from God increase over time. Have you noticed how frequently Jesus challenged the blindness of the religious leaders of His day? The tragedy was that they failed to see their true condition.

> *Then Jesus told him, 'I have come to judge the world. I have come to give sight to the blind and to show those who think they see that they are blind.' The Pharisees who were standing there heard him and asked, 'Are*

[1] G.K. Beale, *We Become What We Worship: A Biblical Theology of Idolatry* (IVP, 2008)

you saying we are blind?' 'If you were blind, you wouldn't be guilty,'
Jesus replied. 'But you remain guilty because you claim you can see.'
(John 9:39–41)

Joshua laid out the options concerning worship very clearly to Israel:

But if you refuse to serve the LORD, then choose today whom you will serve
(Josh. 24:15)

Serving is not optional but what we choose to serve is. Because we are human, we will serve something or someone. The choice of whom or what we will worship, the focus of our service, is the critical choice each of us must make.

PERSONAL EXPLORATION

1. Thinking back over this study series so far, what has been the most challenging discovery for you?

2. Psalm 51 is a psalm of repentance and reaffirmation of commitment to God. If it is appropriate for you, spend time making this psalm your own in prayer.

3. At the core of who you are, what are you worshipping? What are you pouring your energy, gifting, time and resources into? Is there any need for an adjustment here?

4. Spend time reviewing God's faithfulness to you over the years and thank Him for giving you the privilege of serving Him.

STUDYING TOGETHER

1. John 4:19–26 is a part of the encounter between Jesus and a Samaritan woman. Like many people, she believed worship was linked to a location. Jesus opens her eyes to understand that true worship is spiritual. What is your understanding of what Jesus said? How do we worship God in spirit and in truth today?

2. We have been focusing on the fact that what we worship has a transforming influence on our lives for the better or for the worse. Read again the verses found in Romans 12:1–2. How can we be transformed into the people God desires us to become?

    _____

    _____

    _____

    _____

3. 1 Corinthians 10:12–22 contains some solid teaching about temptations, idolatry and the Lord's Supper. What stands out to you as you read this passage?

    _____

    _____

    _____

    _____

4. We considered two of the features of being made in God's likeness – imaging and absorbing. What do we learn about these two qualities from the two passages that were referred to? (1 John 3:1–3; 2 Cor. 3:16–18)

    _____

    _____

    _____

    _____

    _____

APPLYING THE SCRIPTURES

1. How do you respond to the biblical truth that you and I are made in the image of God? Is this a new thought? What does this truth mean for your future possibilities?

    _____

    _____

    _____

    _____

2. What is it in our culture that tends to draw us away from the worship of God? How can we best respond to this?

3. What qualities or behaviour may indicate that a person is keeping the worship of God central in their lives?

4. We can agree that no one is perfect and that sometimes we are very poor reflectors of God's image. How should we address these flaws?

PART FOUR

THRIVING IN OUR PERSONAL TESTS

 PREVIEW

Why what we worship matters

We have emphasised that the biggest decision for any individual is about whom or what we will serve. This statement may seem curious at first glance, but think about it. To have satisfaction in our lives we need to have a sense of purpose. We don't cope well when life has no meaning for us. So people find their purpose in a wide variety of ways. Committed Christians find their meaning in their relationship with God. Others go deep into the deception of other religious traditions. Still others turn to worship darker things and become enslaved by alcohol, drugs, electronic addictions, greed, power, pseudo-religious activities, lust, exercise, food and so on.

Some avid football fans provide an excellent example of modern worship when they become fully absorbed in supporting their team. Some supporters spend many hours watching games and interviews and much of their money buying game tickets and the kits to look exactly like the players of the team they support. They shout with joy when their team does well and some weep if their team loses, or worse, is relegated at the end of the season. They join in with others, singing the team songs with hands raised. This is their life. This is what they worship. Of course not all sport followers are this extreme, but I am sure you get the point. We are worshipping beings. That is part of human uniqueness. We will all worship (serve) one thing or another. If it is not God, then it will be something else. Worship and service are inextricably linked (Rom. 12:1–2).

We have observed that the major offence against God recorded over and over again in the Scriptures is idolatry. Today we in the West may not serve the carved idols that Israel and Judah followed but we may idolise ourselves and become trapped in self-centredness and self-worship. The idol for many today is accumulating more and more wealth or power and this drive to accumulate consumes these people. Jesus made it clear: you cannot serve God and money (Matt. 6:24; Luke 16:13).

One of the clearest teachings Jesus gave that identified His true followers is found in Mark 8:34–38. To follow Jesus and be His disciple is more than church attendance or Bible reading or regular prayer times or keeping the rules of the church. The Pharisees were experts at this type of activity in the Jewish culture but Jesus soundly condemned them for their superficiality. They had the outward show but inwardly their heart and commitment were elsewhere.

Jesus demands all we are, all our focus and all our energy in His service. This is not a call to full time Christian ministry, though this may be true for a minority of today's disciples. It is, rather, a call for each of us to live in responsive obedience to the Holy Spirit in whatever situation and in whatever we do, because of our heartfelt love for God (Matt. 6:21; Luke 12:34; Prov. 4:23). This responsiveness takes place in the middle of our everyday lives.

PERSONAL EXPLORATION

Prayerfully meditate on the Scripture passages below. It is suggested that you invite the Holy Spirit to open your eyes to see what God wants you to understand today about your life's difficult circumstances. You may like to record your thoughts in the spaces provided.

1. James 1:2–8

2. 1 Peter 1:3–7

3. Matthew 6:21; Luke 12:34; Proverbs 4:23

_____

_____

_____

_____

_____

_____

STUDYING TOGETHER

As we come to the final session in this series, four passages are offered
for you to discuss. Each of them contains helpful teaching about the trials
and temptations that we face in life. Let's not forget that at the time the
New Testament was written Christians faced extreme opposition on many
fronts. For many, to be identified as followers of the Way (of Jesus Christ)
could have deadly consequences. Sometimes the writers were addressing
life-threatening circumstances when they spoke and wrote. Because of this,
their words carry added power for us today. What do we learn from the
teaching given here about how our character grows through these trials?

1. John 16:33

_____

_____

_____

_____

_____

_____

2. 1 Peter 5:8–11

_____

_____

_____

_____

_____

_____

3. Romans 5:1–5

4. 2 Corinthians 12:7–10

APPLYING THE SCRIPTURES

1. Perhaps you have one or two in your group who have survived some traumatic times in their lives. What did they learn? What encouragement do they have for the rest of the group?

2. The apostle Paul give us very sound advice concerning how to use any comfort we receive from God as a way of helping others going through their trials (2 Cor. 1:3–5). How can we help anyone who is in the middle of tough times in our group? Be very practical in this. Offer real suggestions for real issues.

_____

_____

_____

_____

_____

3. How can we balance our everyday responsibilities alongside keeping our central focus on God?

_____

_____

_____

_____

4. Does anyone in your group request specific prayer for the battles they are facing right now? Close this session in prayer for one another, if this is appropriate.

_____

_____

_____

_____

_____

APPENDIX:

SURVIVING AND THRIVING THROUGH OUR TRIALS

I find the narrative of Job's trials particularly compelling and challenging. His story, found in the Old Testament book of the same name, is a tragic account of one disaster following hard on the previous one. From being wealthy, prosperous, respected and the head of a significantly large family, his world unravels in a catastrophic way. He loses his possessions and his family and the respect he deserves. What a test of his inner character it was. The loss of his family produces a great outpouring of his grief but his trust in God does not waver.

> *At this, Job got up and tore his robe and shaved his head. Then he fell to the ground in worship and said: 'Naked I came from my mother's womb, and naked I will depart. The LORD gave and the LORD has taken away; may the name of the LORD be praised.' In all this, Job did not sin by charging God with wrongdoing.*
> (Job 1:20–22, NIV)

His physical health crumbles and he becomes a tragic shadow of his former self. To add to his woes God seems to have disappeared from his life. Former friends harass him because they wrongly interpret the cause of his many trials as God's punishment for Job's sins. Their unhelpful comments add unjust emotional pain and isolation to his other losses.

In the end, of course, God vindicates Job. He is blessed more than before through the personal restitution of status, of a new family and in abundant material blessings. Yet we know from our own experiences that the memories of his painful past experiences would remain deeply etched in the depths of his being. They would never go away. Like Jacob, after his struggle with God at the Jabbok River, he walked with a permanent inner 'limp' (Gen. 32:22–32). Job had suffered physically, relationally and emotionally. But out of the inner scars, his character and standing increased. He received applause from God and praise from those who knew him.

But, as with us, an unanswered question probably remained. Why did God allow this to happen to me? Perhaps Job was clearer as the dark clouds of suffering were swept away and he looked back over the devastating episodes in his life. I believe it is more likely that he did not have many of his 'why' questions answered. For Job, it was enough that his faithful God had never abandoned him.

Your story and mine are not like Job's. Each of our personal journeys will be very different from each other. Perhaps as you read this you are thinking of the really tough events in your own past or present life. Maybe you are wondering why God has permitted you to face these tests. Perhaps you believe He has abandoned you. The ultimate question we each face in these trying times concerns where we will put our trust. Comparing our tough life story to the stories of others can easily lead us into self-pity and bitterness. It is the natural route downward. If we do not look higher to God and deeper into our status as God's children, we can sink down under the weight of the trials we face. Left to our own ideas and resources life can become a daily, hopeless burden. Like Job, our worship of God gives us a focus and power beyond our own resources and provides a flame of hope for our futures.

In 1 Corinthians 10:13, the apostle Paul emphasises that temptations are common experiences for all human beings but also that God sets the boundaries and will not allow testing to go beyond our capacity to come through these trials victoriously and stronger. Essentially, testing is to demonstrate how *good* we may become, not how *bad* we have been. Every time we triumph in testing times we release applause from heaven and our character grows. We become more personally and spiritually mature. We become wiser and more whole through each success. By overcoming these trials we confirm our true identity as children of the King of kings. God's kids have the power to survive and thrive as a result of testing times. With God's help, these testing times are able to build us up rather than break us down.

The ultimate issue in our tests and trials is always about who or what we will worship. In our raw pain we face critical questions. How will we handle these trials? How will we respond to God in the middle of our suffering and uncertainty? Will we allow God to use the painful times to transform us more and more into the person He desires us to become?

With God's help, may you survive and thrive.

QUESTIONS WORTH CONSIDERING WHEN WE ARE ENDURING DIFFICULT TRIALS OR TEMPTATIONS

It is not unusual for people to go through trying times without reflecting on key questions that may help them to endure the unwelcome experience and lead them towards the most positive outcome possible. In contemplating these questions we should not overlook the fact that in many difficult times we simply have to grit our teeth and forge ahead through the pain and confusion. Often any benefits can only be seen after a significant period of time has passed. Then there are those other experiences that we never do understand, and we never recognise any benefits because the hurt is so intense or because the painful effects are so enduring. These are the times when our faith in God's love for us is paramount.

These questions are offered primarily for personal reflection; however, you may choose to consider them privately or use them in the context of your small group.

Am I centred on Christ for my guidance and strength or do I rely for the most part on my own resources and wisdom during trails and temptations?

To what extent am I using my spiritual resources (Bible study, prayer, meditation, silence, worship and so on) to strengthen me during trials and temptations?

Is this particular trial avoidable and if so, should I avoid it?

Is this trial my own fault or is it entirely outside my control?

To what extent do I have an objective view of the trial I am facing? (It is so easy to ignore the helpful perspective of others we know.)

How can I best manage any stress, pain or uncertainty that accompanies this trial?

How much does this particular trial affect other people, such as my close friends and family?

Does this trial mean that there will be a permanent change in my life or is it only temporary?

Do I have a support network that I can turn to for advice and encouragement?

What can I learn as I go through this trial? (Don't waste your sorrows.) What can I hope to learn from this experience?

What would be the best outcome for me should I come through this trial or temptation well?

NATIONAL DISTRIBUTORS

UK: (and countries not listed below)

CWR, Waverley Abbey House, Waverley Lane, Farnham, Surrey GU9 8EP.

Tel: (01252) 784700 Outside UK (44) 1252 784700 Email: mail@cwr.org.uk

AUSTRALIA: KI Entertainment, Unit 21 317-321 Woodpark Road, Smithfield, New South Wales 2164
Tel: 1 800 850 777 Fax: 02 9604 3699 Email: sales@kientertainment.com.au

CANADA: David C Cook Distribution Canada, PO Box 98, 55 Woodslee Avenue, Paris, Ontario N3L
3E5 Tel: 1800 263 2664 Email: joy.kearley@davidccook.ca

GHANA: Challenge Enterprises of Ghana, PO Box 5723, Accra
Tel: (021) 222437/223249 Fax: (021) 226227 Email: ceg@africaonline.com.gh

HONG KONG: Cross Communications Ltd, 11/F Ko's House, 577 Nathan Road, Kowloon
Tel: 2780 1188 Fax: 2770 6229 Email: cross@crosshk.com

INDIA: Crystal Communications, Plot No. 125, Road No. 7, T.M.C, Mahendra Hills, East Marredpally,
Secunderabad - 500026 Tel/Fax: (040) 27737145 Email: crystal_edwj@rediffmail.com

KENYA: Keswick Books and Gifts Ltd, PO Box 10242-00400, Nairobi
Tel: (020) 2226047/312639 Email: sales.keswick@africaonline.co.ke

MALAYSIA: Canaanland Distributors Sdn Bhd, No. 25 Jalan PJU 1A/41B, NZX Commercial Centre,
Ara Jaya, 47301 Petaling Jaya, Selangor
Tel: (03) 7885 0540/1/2 Fax: (03) 7885 0545 Email: info@canaanland.com.my

Salvation Publishing & Distribution Sdn Bhd, 23 Jalan SS 2/64, 47300 Petaling Jaya, Selangor
Tel: (03) 78766411/78766797 Fax: (03) 78757066/78756360 Email: info@salvationbookcentre.com

NEW ZEALAND: KI Entertainment, Unit 21 317-321 Woodpark Road, Smithfield, New South Wales
2164, Australia Tel: 0 800 850 777 Fax: +612 9604 3699 Email: sales@kientertainment.com.au

NIGERIA: FBFM, Helen Baugh House, 96 St Finbarr's College Road, Akoka, Lagos
Tel: (+234) 01-7747429, 08075201777, 08186337699, 08154453905 Email: fbfm_1@yahoo.com

PHILIPPINES: OMF Literature Inc, 776 Boni Avenue, Mandaluyong City
Tel: (02) 531 2183 Fax: (02) 531 1960 Email: gloadlaon@omflit.com

SINGAPORE: Alby Commercial Enterprises Pte Ltd, 95 Kallang Avenue #04-00, AIS Industrial
Building, 339420 Tel: (+65) 629 27238 Fax: (+65) 629 27235 Email: marketing@alby.com.sg

SOUTH AFRICA: Life Media & Distribution, Unit 20, Tungesten Industrial Park, 7 C R Swart Drive,
Strydompark 2125 Tel: (+27) 0117924277 Fax: (+27) 0117924512 Email: orders@lifemedia.co.za

SRI LANKA: Christombu Publications (Pvt) Ltd, Bartleet House, 65 Braybrooke Place, Colombo 2
Tel: (+941) 2421073/2447665 Email: christombupublications@gmail.com

USA: David C Cook Distribution Canada, PO Box 98, 55 Woodslee Avenue, Paris, Ontario N3L 3E5,
Canada Tel: 1800 263 2664 Email: joy.kearley@davidccook.ca

CWR is a Registered Charity – Number 294387
CWR is a Limited Company registered in England – Registration Number 1990308

WHO DO YOU THINK YOU ARE?

Our true identity in Christ is something that is to be greatly celebrated and valued. In this insightful study guide, Ron Kallmier encourages us to renew our minds and question our core beliefs. Based on key Old and New Testament passages, this booklet is designed for use by individuals and small groups.

Identity
48 pages, paperback, 210mm x 148mm
ISBN: 978-1-78259-235-8

Hearing God
ISBN: 978-1-85345-764-7

Strong Faith for Tough Times
ISBN: 978-1-78259-054-5

Discovering Your Spiritual Gifts
ISBN: 978-1-85345-765-4

Guidance
ISBN: 978-1-78259-053-8

smallGroup central

ALL OF OUR SMALL GROUP IDEAS AND RESOURCES IN ONE PLACE.

Small Group Central is packed with clear, easy to use, inspiration for your group. You will find:

- **Free teaching:** Andy Peck, a CWR tutor, has created videos on the practicalities of leading a small group

- **Free tools:** templates, discussion starters, icebreakers – all you need to lead a group study effectively

- **Resources:** books, booklets and DVDs on an extensive list of themes, Bible books and life issues.

Log on and find out more at
www.smallgroupcentral.org.uk

40 DAYS WITH JESUS

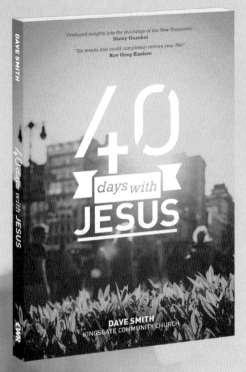

'Profound insights into the teachings of the New Testament.'
Nicky Gumbel

'Six weeks that could completely restore your life!'
Rev Greg Haslam

DAVE SMITH
KINGSGATE COMMUNITY CHURCH

Also available in eBook formats

For Individuals:
Be strengthened as you read this 40-day devotional exploring the life-changing encounters biblical characters had with the risen Jesus.

For Small Groups:
Free online videos and study guides to help small groups learn and share together as they work through the 40-day devotional.

For Churches:
Free online sermon outlines for church leaders exploring each of the 6 encounters highlighted in the devotional and small group resources.

Bulk buy available for small groups and churches.

ISBN: 978-1-78259-138-2

Dave Smith is one of the most inspirational Christian leaders in the UK today. I am delighted that through this book he has given us not only profound insights into the teachings of the New Testament but helped each of us draw daily closer to Jesus Christ.

NICKY GUMBEL

For more information visit **www.40days.info** or call **01252 784700**

Courses and seminars

Publishing and media

Conference facilities

Transforming lives

CWR's vision is to enable people to experience personal transformation through applying God's Word to their lives and relationships.

Our Bible-based training and resources help people around the world to:
• Grow in their walk with God
• Understand and apply Scripture to their lives
• Resource themselves and their church
• Develop pastoral care and counselling skills
• Train for leadership
• Strengthen relationships, marriage and family life and much more.

Our insightful writers provide daily Bible reading notes and other resources for all ages, and our experienced course designers and presenters have gained an international reputation for excellence and effectiveness.

CWR's Training and Conference Centres in Surrey and East Sussex, England, provide excellent facilities in idyllic settings – ideal for both learning and spiritual refreshment.

CWR Applying God's Word
to everyday life and relationships

CWR, Waverley Abbey House,
Waverley Lane, Farnham,
Surrey GU9 8EP, UK

Telephone: +44 (0)1252 784700
Email: info@cwr.org.uk
Website: www.cwr.org.uk

Registered Charity No 294387
Company Registration No 1990308